I HATE ANN COULTER!

I HATE ANN COULTER!

by **UNANIMOUS**

SIMON SPOTLIGHT ENTERTAINMENT
New York | London | Toronto | Sydney

SIMON SPOTLIGHT ENTERTAINMENT
An imprint of Simon & Schuster
1230 Avenue of the Americas, New York, New York 10020
SIMON SPOTLIGHT ENTERTAINMENT and related logo are trademarks
of Simon & Schuster, Inc.
Designed by Steve Kennedy
Manufactured in the United States of America
First Edition   10 9 8 7 6 5 4
Library of Congress Cataloging-in-Publication Data
I hate Ann Coulter / Unanimous.—1st ed.
p. cm.
ISBN-13: 978-1-4169-3659-6
ISBN-10: 1-4169-3659-9
1. Coulter, Ann H.
PN4874.C743I2 2007
818'.602—dc22
2006027196

For Ann, whom we love
"like O.J. loved Nicole"

"Her books are filled with lies, slander and phony foot-notes that are themselves lies and slanders."

—ERIC ALTERMAN, *The Nation*

"My track record is pretty good on predictions.[1]"

—ANN COULTER, *Rivera Live* DECEMBER 8, 1998

---

[1] "I think [Whitewater's] going to prevent the first lady from running for Senate." —Ann Coulter, *Rivera Live*, March 12, 1999

Table of Contents

Preface: Searching Ann Coulter   1

Part 1: **I Am a Fan of the First Amendment, but I Still
Think We Should Flog Her on Live Television**   3

Reasons I Hate Ann Coulter   6

Ann Coulter 101   7

Thanks to My Public School Teachers, I'm
Just Too Dumb to Get Her (and So Are You)   9

What I Learned in Public School,
Part I: No Name-Calling   11

What I Learned in Public School,
Part II: Eyes on Your Own Paper   12

Chapman v. Coulter   13

If at First You're Called a Cheat, Lie, Lie Again   15

The Cost of Plagiarism   17

Returning *High Crimes* to Borders   17

What I Learned in Public School,
Part III: Check Your Facts   18

Match These Nutcases with the Writings
They Authored   19

Ann Coulter Lies   20

Should Ann Be in Jail?   21

Coulter v. Coulter   23

I'm Serious, Bust Her Ass!   24

Ann's Fetish for Slick Willie   28

The Devil and Miss Jones:
The Ann and Paula Story   30

Pop Quiz: Ann Coulter or Adolf Hitler?   32

Bathhouse Annie   33

Confessions of an al-Pieda Terrorist   35

Tofu Terror Pie   40

Black Tuesday   41

Exclusive! No Sympathy for the
She-Devil from Pastor Harry   42

Not Such a *Godless* World After All   46

When Annimals Attack   47

The Anntichrist   48

Part 2:   **How to Get Rid of a Political Bunny Boiler**   49

Dumping Ann   51

I Hate Ann Coulter, and So Do You   54

Melannoma   55

A Thousand Points of Light   56

Jimmy Carter Will Beat Your Ass   58

Let My People Go   60

What's So Funny About War, Hate, and
Condescension?   63

Canada to Ann: *Je vous deteste!*   66

Do Ann's Books Cause Global Warming?   68

Variations on "I Hate Ann Coulter"   69

Students Risk Being Called "Ugly Gay Fetus Killers"   70

Dame Coulter?   71

Pop Quiz: Ann Coulter or Ted Nugent?   71

The Ann Coulter Movie Guide   72

How to Talk to Ann (If You Must)   73

Liberal Education   76

New Canaan Syndrome   79

In and Out of Love   81

How to Talk Like a Porn Star   82

On Being Ann Coulter   84

Femannism   86

Coultourettes   87

Half Baked   88

We D.A.R.E. You   90

Darwin/Win   92

CoulterCard   92

Brassball   93

Ann Coulter-Robertson   94

You're Too Into Ann If . . .   96

Inner Beauty   97

The Baby Seal Book Club   98

Point/Coulterpoint   101

Casting Ann Coulter   102

The Sound and the Furry   103

Best. Interview. Ever.   104

New Canaan High, Class of '80   105

Male Bag   107

Can You Be Like Ann?   110

The Blair Bitch Project   111

What Would Ann Do?   112

Apocryphal Ann   113

Early Coulter Book Discovered   115

Afterword: A Letter from Unanimous   116

Preface:
Searching Ann Coulter

Late one night after watching Fox News, I Googled the phrase "I Hate Ann Coulter" and got back 19,100 results in 0.30 seconds.

I thought, *What's the rush, Google? Why not slow down and do a more thorough job?*

This highly scientific research proved that Ann Coulter had made a lot of enemies over the years. But then came her "Black Tuesday" (6/6/06) *Today* show appearance, when she stopped pushing the envelope and simply set it on fire—by spitting venomous accusations at the 9/11 widows (aka the "Jersey Girls"). That day I could feel America changing. We were rallying together, seeking a community of like-minded people, looking for help in a common cause. It was time to get Ann Coulter out of our lives.

To that end, here is the Ann haters' handbook of sanity, our crib sheet to telling Ann lovers to cork their pieholes.

Part 1:

I Am a Fan of the First Amendment, but I Still Think We Should Flog Her on Live Television

"[Ann Coulter] is one of the most toxic people on the American cultural scene. . . . There's no point in giving her more oxygen to consume."

—ARIANNA HUFFINGTON,
NATIONAL SOCIETY OF NEWSPAPER COLUMNISTS,
JULY 1, 2006

Presumably, Arianna meant metaphorical oxygen. But how about the real stuff? Let's stop giving Ann our perfectly good American oxygen, and maybe she'll leave. Or better yet, let's take a nod from David Blaine and suspend her in an oxygenless tank above Rockefeller Plaza and broadcast her slow death on the *Today* show. I'm positive that Katie Couric would be willing to make a reunion cameo for the segment.

Reasons I Hate Ann Coulter

1. She says, "Frankly, I'm not a big fan of the First Amendment," but she never shuts up.

2. She boasts, "I've never had bulimia!" while obviously anorexic.

3. She says, "It's my total slutty look" as though she had another one.

4. She claims that God looked down on her and said, "We've got enough lawyers. I'm putting you on TV," ignoring that her existence proves there is no God.

5. She argues that Bill Clinton is gay because "that sort of rampant [heterosexual] promiscuity does show some level of latent homosexuality" but ignores that her own rampant vagina does show she's a man.

6. She calls *Today* show host Katie Couric "the affable Eva Braun of morning TV." What exactly does she mean by "affable"?

7. She calls Pamela Harriman and Patricia Duff "whores," but she arrives at the *Today* show at 6:00 a.m. in last night's cocktail dress.

8. She clogs the toilet, claiming, "Because of liberal government bureaucrats, they decided that we can only have two tablespoons of water in the toilet. You throw half a tissue in the toilet and you have to flush it sixteen times." Yeah right.

Ann Coulter 101

Her Original Claim to Fame: Volunteered as a legal adviser for attorneys representing Paula Jones in her sexual harassment case against President Bill Clinton. Jones's case was eventually dismissed[2].

She Was Fired: From MSNBC after telling a disabled Vietnam vet antiwar activist that "people like you caused us to lose that war."

Her Column Was Dropped: By *National Review*, in 2001, after she responded to the 9/11 attacks in a column by writing, "We should invade their countries, kill their leaders and convert them to Christianity."

Her Column Was Dropped Again: By Tucson's *Arizona Daily Star*, whose editor explained, "We've decided that syndicated columnist Ann Coulter has worn out her welcome. Many readers find her shrill, bombastic and mean-spirited."

[2.] In 2002, Jones boxed ex-skater Tonya Harding on Fox TV's *Celebrity Boxing*.

Favorite Bands: The Grateful Dead, String Cheese Incident, Phish, Dave Matthews Band, Blues Traveler, New Potato Caboose. (Maybe she damaged her brain doing all that hippie twirling?)

> For discussion: Does Ann pee standing up?

Thanks to My Public School Teachers, I'm Just Too Dumb to Get Her (and So Are You)

ANN COULTER: *No, I'm saying—I'm merely—I'm saying what I'm saying. I don't know why I'm always having people say, are you trying to say—you know what you can do if you want to know what I'm saying is listen to what I'm saying. What I'm saying is what I said. . . .*

TUCKER CARLSON: *I tried that . . . I couldn't understand.*

—Crossfire, JUNE 28, 2002

Ann has written five books, and they have all gone straight to the top of bestseller lists. However, I don't think anyone reads them.

Her critics take ill after a chapter or two. Reviewing Ann's book *Treason* in the *Washington Times,* Hoover Institution conservative Arnold Beichman wrote that he "tried to read Miss Coulter's book and failed." Maybe we're all just too dumb to get Ann.

I find her books as inscrutable as a shrieking drunk outside a bar at two in the morning—and far less charming.

Maybe the reason I'm too stupid to get Ann is because I was educated in public schools. So were the majority of Americans, including you most likely. According to Ann, public school teachers are "taxpayer-supported parasites."

In *Godless*, Ann accuses every public school teacher of "inculcating students in the precepts of the Socialist Party of America—as understood by retarded people." She bases her argument on one tenth-grade geography teacher in Colorado who criticized President Bush in the course of a lecture. Ann quotes the teacher saying to his students, "What I'm trying to get you to do is think more in depth."

Who wants a teacher like that?

I don't really remember being inculcated in the precepts of the Socialist Party, do you? Instead, at my public school the teachers taught us to not call one another names and to make sure our facts were accurate (I guess Ann was more interested in "creative" writing). They also taught us to not copy other people's work.

What I Learned in Public School, Part I: No Name-Calling

Ann said, "Arguments by name-calling, rather than truth and light, can generally be presumed fraudulent." Later Ann said about the 9/11 widows, "Harpies and witches is what I think they are, which is why I used those words. . . . I'd say my 'name-calling' has been a smashing success. And by the way, I've got a few more names in my bag." So have we, Ann!

Some Things to Call Ann:
- Ann Cold Sore
- The Whore of Babble On
- Anndolf Coultler
- The Anntichrist
- Right-Wing Telebimbo
- Ano Coulter
- Man Coulter
- Coultergeist
- Self-Aggrandizing PR Slut

What I Learned in Public School, Part II: Eyes on Your Own Paper

In December 1998, three months after *High Crimes and Misdemeanors* was first published, former *Human Events* Clinton reporter Michael Chapman groused to his bosses that material he'd prepared for a 1997 article titled "A Case for Impeachment" ran close to verbatim or was paraphrased without citation in Ann's book. "Furthermore," he added, "mostly all of chapter 18, 'Wampumgate,' is a rewrite or paraphrase of reporting I did for *HE*."

According to the *Boston Globe*, which broke the story, Chapman had originally been approached about ghost-writing the book for Ann, but that job went to former *Insight* writer David Wagner, who produced a first draft that was rejected for not bitch slapping the president in Ann's vicious manner. Ann then single-handedly wrote the book after reading both Chapman's and Wagner's work.

"They offered some basis for source material, but it was my impression that she threw those drafts away as irrelevant," Regnery's executive editor Harry Crocker told *Globe* reporter Alex Beam in defending Ann. "[If you compare the two], she thinks you wouldn't find any overlap. The book is 100 percent Ann Coulter."

Here are the passages Beam cited. You decide.

CHAPMAN V. COULTER

MICHAEL CHAPMAN, "A Case for Impeachment," *Human Events*, (5/23/97)

ANN COULTER, *High Crimes and Misdemeanors* (Regnery, 1998)

CHAPMAN, page 13: *"Four Democratic fundraisers have stated that former DNC Finance Chairman Marvin Rosen explicitly advocated selling access to the President."*

COULTER, page 219: *"At least four Democratic fund-raising officials have revealed that former DNC Finance Chairman Marvin Rosen explicitly advocated selling access to the president."*

* * * * * * * * * * * *

CHAPMAN, page 13: *"A DNC fundraiser told Nynex executives they would receive invitations to White House 'coffees' if they joined the DNC's 'Managing Trustees' program and agreed to donate $100,000."*

COULTER, page 219: *"A DNC fund-raiser told Nynex Corporation executives that they would receive invitations to White House coffees if they joined the DNC's 'Managing Trustees' program and agreed to donate $100,000."*

· · · · · · · · · · · · ·

CHAPMAN, page 28: *"Harry Thomason, the Hollywood TV executive famous for producing 'Evening Shade' and "Designing Women' ... He is an old friend of Bill and Hillary Clinton, having first met the future President when Thomason was a high school football coach in the 1970s in Arkansas. . . . Thomason, meanwhile, started to spread rumors about the Travel Office."*

COULTER, page 121: *"Harry Thomason, the Hollywood television executive famous for producing such shows as* Evening Shade *and* Designing Women, *was a major Clinton fund-raiser. He is an old friend of Bill and Hillary Clinton, having first met the future president when Thomason was an Arkansas high school football coach in the 1970s. . . . Thomason spread rumors about the Travel Office."*

If at First You're Called a Cheat, Lie, Lie Again

Did Ann learn her lesson? Of course not. She went on to plagiarize parts of *Godless*! A clever reporter at the *New York Post*, Philip Recchia, asked John Barrie, CEO of iParadigms and creator of a top plagiarism-recognition software, to go through *Godless* and the last twelve months of her columns. Barrie's review found three "textbook instances of plagiarism" in *Godless* as well as numerous "verbatim lifts" in her weekly syndicated column. According to Recchia's story, three different passages varying between twenty-five and thirty-three words in length appeared in three different sources prior to the release of Ann's book. As the Web site Media Matters concluded, basically, she stole from Planned Parenthood literature (oh the irony), the *San Francisco Chronicle*, and Maine's *Portland Press Herald*.

Barrie also found sloppy work in Ann's citations and columns, though he said he and his staff didn't make it through all of her columns. "We'd seen enough," he explained. Barrie termed it the "stuff that would flunk any English student."

Ann's publisher, Crown Forum, and the syndicator of her daily column, Universal Press, expressed their support and said they did not find any merits to warrant further investigation.

In her June 14, 2006, column, Ann talks about facts universally accepted:

✒ She says it's a fact that liberals are godless.

✒ She says it's a fact that Bill Clinton is a rapist.

According to John Barrie's review of her work, she can add another fact to her list: Ann Coulter is a plagiarist. Oh, wait. That would actually be true, so never mind.

I'd like Ann to write a letter of apology to former *New York Times* plagiarist Jayson Blair for all the nasty things she said about him as his sorry life and once-promising career came undone. And I want the letter to be *all her own work.*

THE COST OF PLAGIARISM[3]

JAYSON BLAIR: plagiarism and fabrication . . . resigned from *New York Times*.

Jack Kelley: possible plagiarism and fabrication . . . resigned from *USA Today*.

RICK BRAGG: used intern's reporting without attribution . . . resigned from *New York Times*.

MICHAEL BOLTON: plagiarism of "Love Is a Wonderful Thing" by the Isley Brothers . . . ordered to pay $5.4 million.

ANN COULTER: plagiarism and sloppy attribution. . . . Ann calls the *New York Post* "a tabloid," which it has always admitted proudly, and continues to write books.

RETURNING *HIGH CRIMES* TO BORDERS

I walked into my local Borders with my original hardcover in hand and showed it to the pleasant-looking woman at the register.

ME: I'd like to return this book, *High Crimes and Misdemeanors*.

SALESPERSON: Is there a reason?

ME: I'd rather give my money to the authors of the original material, which she plagiarized. Plus, I hate Ann Coulter.

SALESPERSON: I hate her too. Don't tell my husband, but I'd like to put a hit on her.

---

[3]. From famousplagiarists.com. See, Ann, it's easy!

What I Learned in Public School, Part III: Check Your Facts

With *Slander* barely on the shelves, online critics (spinsanity.com, Scoobie Davis Online, and dailyhowler.com) brilliantly and accurately ripped Ann for errors, hyperbole, and gross misrepresentations. In a story titled "How Slippery Is *Slander*?" the vaunted *Columbia Journalism Review* reported that Ann's publisher, Crown Forum, revised the second edition by correcting five errors, three minor misidentifications of public figures, a wrong claim about press coverage of an Al Gore mistake, and a doozy of a gaffe about the coverage of Dale Earnhardt's death in the *New York Times*—all of which undermined Ann's credibility.

The *CJR* also looked into forty other alleged mistakes, such as this one:

COULTER CLAIM: Liberals called the American flag "very, very dumb." (p. 4)

FOOTNOTE: She cites a *New York Times* story in which a liberal history professor, Daniel Boylan, makes no claim about the intelligence of the flag. He does criticize—as "acting very, very dumb in their patriotism"—those who have criticized Hawaii for not flying an American flag over Iolani Palace, the nineteenth century seat of the Hawaiian monarchy.

In his exhaustive analysis of Coulter's work, Scoobie Davis highlights her typical smears (e.g., "an attack on America by fanatical Muslims had finally provided liberals with a religion they could respect") and their underlying groundlessness. "Again, Coulter provides no examples of a single liberal who hated religion prior to 9/11 and then who embraced radical Islam after 9/11."

MATCH THESE NUTCASES WITH THE WRITINGS THEY AUTHORED

1. Adolf Hitler
2. Theodore Kaczynski
3. Charles Manson
4. David Duke
5. Ann Coulter

A. *Liberty, Art, and Nationhood*
B. *Without Conscience*
C. *My Awakening*
D. "Answering My Critics"
E. "Industrial Society and Its Future"

Answer key: 1. A, 2. E, 3. B, 4. C, 5. D

Ann Coulter Lies

In 2002, Ann claimed to several journalists, including Aileen Jacobson of *Newsday* and Toby Harnden of the London *Telegraph*, that she was thirty-eight years old, not forty years old as their research indicated.

"An air of mystery surrounds Coulter's age," Harnden wrote.

The contradiction ignited a controversy. "Is Human Uzi Ann Coulter 38 or 40 years old?" wrote then *Washington Post* reporter Lloyd Grove in a September 2002 follow-up. "And when she insists that she's the former, is she telling a fib?" The *Washington Post,* the paper that broke Watergate, threw its investigative muscle into the case and discovered a discrepancy.

According to Grove, Ann's Connecticut driver's license and voter registration card listed her birthday as December 8, 1961. However, her Washington, D.C., driver's license had her born in 1963. Which is it? There is only one conceivable theory that can save Ann's integrity: While science has proven human beings are born just once, the religious Right—a group with which Ann is closely aligned—maintains a person can be *born again*.

Should Ann Be in Jail?

When Lloyd Grove reached her, Ann insisted she was thirty-eight. A trained lawyer, Ann didn't seem to care about the ramifications of that response. But since Connecticut records showed that she had registered to vote in 1980, that meant she had voted at age sixteen and driven at age fourteen. Both illegal acts. If she was indeed forty, as public records indicated, she had lied on her D.C. driver's license—yet another crime: forgery on a government document.

In early 2006, Palm Beach County's supervisor of elections began investigating Ann on allegations of voter fraud, as if Florida could afford another voter fraud incident concerning a prominent Republican. But *Palm Beach Post* reporter Jose Lambiet broke the story, reporting that Ann may have committed a third-degree felony by knowingly writing down an incorrect address on her Palm Beach voter registration form and then casting "her ballot in a precinct 4 miles north of the precinct where she owns a home—and that could be a big no-no."

On the voter registration form, she used her real estate agent's address and signed the form, stating that all the information was true under the penalty of law (said law being a third-degree felony). That could mean a $5,000 fine and up to five years in the slammer. While Palm Beach election officials investigated Ann and considered erasing her from voter rolls until she re-registered with truthful information, Ann behaved with the self-righteous condescension typical of holier-than-thou right-wingers who behave as if the law of the land applies to everyone but them.[4]

During a Q&A period at a college lecture, a student asked Ann about "allegations that you knowingly voted in the wrong precinct in Palm Beach."

"No, I don't live in Palm Beach," shot Ann. "Maybe you shouldn't read retarded news!"

If Ann doesn't "live in Palm Beach" (her words), what the heck was she doing registering to vote there (her signature)?

---

[4] See President Richard Nixon, Rev. Jim Baker, Jimmy Swaggart, Sen. Tom DeLaly, etc.

COULTER V. COULTER

Imagine Ann the attorney in court questioning Ann the defendant:

ATTORNEY COULTER: On one document you said you were born in 1961. On another you said it was 1963. Which is correct?

DEFENDANT COULTER: Bite me, you Alger Hiss–loving Clinton wannabe.

ATTORNEY COULTER: In other words, you're a liar.

DEFENDANT COULTER: There you go with the name-calling that liberals always resort to.

ATTORNEY COULTER: If you lie about your age and where you vote, how do we know you aren't lying about President Clinton masturbating in the sink, liberals being godless, public school teachers being parasites, and everything else you've maintained as fact?

DEFENDANT COULTER: I have endnotes!

I'm Serious, Bust Her Ass!

On July 20, 2006, the world became safer for Bill Clinton. That day James L. Williford, a fifty-seven-year-old resident of Oklahoma City, was indicted by authorities for allegedly making threatening remarks about Clinton. According to reports, three employees at the Edwards Chiropractic Clinic claimed they heard Williford threaten to "bust a cap" at Clinton. Williford, who could get five years in prison and be fined $250,000, denied the allegations, though he acknowledged believing the former president was "a communist mole for the Red Chinese."

These kind of threats are routine for the nation's police departments and the Secret Service. They usually result in an arrest.

In September 2004, Dade County, Florida, authorities arrested Roberto Rodriguez, a homeless man, after he threatened President Bush and his brother, Florida governor Jeb Bush, via e-mails sent from the public library. In messages addressed to the White House, FBI, CIA, and the Florida governor's office, Rodriguez admitted he wanted to "burn the ass of the president" and take out the governor.

In February 2001, a Secret Service agent shot Robert Pickett, a forty-seven-year-old from Indiana, in the knee after he waved a loaded handgun near the White House.

In December 1996, Rev. Rob Shenck was detained by Secret Service agents for shouting at President Clinton, "God will hold you to account, Mr. President," during a Christmas Eve service at the Washington National Cathedral.

And so on. You get the point. The Secret Service is on the job and set to pounce. Law enforcement has a lot of leeway in terms of whom they can go after, and they are supposed to be more careful than not. For good reason.

Consider these statistics to date:

- One out of ten U.S. presidents has been assassinated.
- One other president was shot but not fatally.
- Eleven other presidents were uninjured in failed assassination attempts.

Ann has made a lot of threats. In January 2006, when she was speaking at Philander Smith College, she called for the murder of Supreme Court Justice John Paul Stevens. She said, "We need somebody to put rat poisoning in Justice Stevens's crème brûlée." Ann immediately added that her comment was "a joke, for you in the media." However, it's as against the law to threaten the life of a Supreme Court justice as it is to threaten a U.S. president, and that's exactly what Ann did.

Why wasn't she arrested? Seriously, her remarks were more direct and threatening than Rev. Shenck's, and he was put under the harsh light by authorities. Why not Ann?

She's on record urging bombings, shootings, torture, and floggings. Ted Kaczynski wrote with the same mad passion and conviction as Ann. Look what happened. Call her the "Loony-Bomber." I want to know why she isn't interrogated like the other wingnuts who threaten government officials.

Joe LaSorsa is CEO of the private Florida-based security firm J.A. LaSorsa and a former Secret Service agent with more than twenty years' experience, including presidential protection detail. He is a serious man with a black-and-white take on morons who say they want to kill government officials. "Just because she's a TV commentator and popular author doesn't give her special privilege to make threats," he said.

Do you consider her dangerous?

"I don't know much about her. If I was the agent on protective detail and I heard that she said she wanted to poison someone, I'd refer her to the proper division. These things go through protocol. Threats are investigated—even innocuous threats. Then an assessment is made."

Can you give me your assessment?

"I think her statements should at the least be dealt with administratively. Let me put it this way. What if you hear a kid at a college say he wants to blow up the science building on campus, but then he says he was joking? What if it turns out he wasn't joking? To be safe, you have to look into these kinds of things—even if they're coming from someone on TV."

I say bust her ass!

Ann's Fetish for Slick Willie

Ann said, "Bill Clinton is in love with the erect penis."

But so is Ann. Make no mistake about that; but it's not just any erect penis. Ann Coulter loves Bill Clinton's erect penis. She actually may love Bill's penis more than he does, and she's more focused on it than Monica Lewinsky ever was. If not for Bill Clinton's penis, Ann might even have gotten a boyfriend by now.

Her first book, *High Crimes and Misdemeanors*, wouldn't exist without Bill's penis. It reads like an ex-girlfriend's obsessive screed after she catches him with someone younger and prettier than her. Like a spurned lover, Ann has trashed Clinton at every opportunity:

 "[Bill Clinton] masturbates in the sinks."

 "We're now at the point that it's beyond whether or not [Bill Clinton] is a horny hick. I really think it's a question of his mental stability. He really could be a lunatic. I think it is a rational question for Americans to ask whether their president is insane."

🖋 "[Bill Clinton] was a very good rapist."

🖋 "If you don't hate Bill Clinton and the people who labored to keep him in office, you don't love your country."

🖋 She has also referred to him as the "Caligula Administration," "IMPOTUS,[5]" and "the felon."

Monica got off sucking Clinton, Ann gets aroused saying "Clinton sucks." It's a fixation. Years have passed since he was in office, and she still writes about him. He's referred to on fifteen pages in her latest book, *Godless*.

I think Ann wants his attention, his love, and his pork sword. Monica's infamous blue dress was from The Gap, had long sleeves, a collar, and buttons down the front. She described it as a work dress, and nothing about it said "hot" or "sexy." Ann often dresses for work in a black mini. She's working it. The outfit, the focus on Clinton's penis—it all seems so transparent. Bill, I think she's ready for you. But heed this warning: Her penis might be bigger than yours.

---

[5] POTUS—President of the United States

The Devil and Miss Jones:
The Ann and Paula Story

Abstract: Every so often a love story enters our hearts and becomes an experience we'll never forget. This is not that story. It's a true tale of how politics, lust, and greed bring two attention-hungry fuglies together in an effort to topple the U.S. presidency.

At thirty-three, Ann Coulter, an ambitious lawyer in Washington, D.C., can't stop thinking about the brilliant, handsome, charismatic U.S. president she has lusted after for more than a decade.

At twenty-eight, former Arkansas state employee Paula Jones files a sexual harassment suit against that same chief executive, claiming that three years earlier he'd propositioned her in a hotel room.

Plot Points:

✎ Jealous that she was not invited to caress this powerful man's bent penis, Coulter wheedles her way onto Jones's legal team and secretly sabotages efforts to settle the case by leaking information about his "distinguishing characteristic." She claims she wants to get the president, when she really wants to get on top of him.

✎ Jones's case is dismissed, and she settles for $850,000, most of which goes to pay legal expenses. Broke and exploited by the president's Republican foes, Jones poses for *Playboy* and *Penthouse* and boxes disgraced ice-skater Tonya Harding on TV.

✎ Coulter, sad, disappointed, and hurt by the woman she once called a "hero," denounces Jones as a "fraud, at least to the extent of pretending to be an honorable and moral person."

✎ In the ensuing months and years Coulter cannot stop thinking, writing, or talking about the president who refused to notice her. While Jones remarries and has children, Coulter's life turns into an obsession, and triumph is transformed into a tragedy you'll never forget.

See the movie the *Rocky Mountain News* calls "Girls Gone Vile!"

POP QUIZ: ANN COULTER OR ADOLF HITLER?

Identify who said the following statements: **Ann Coulter** or **Adolf Hitler**.

1. "As a Christian . . . I have the duty to be a fighter for truth and justice."
2. "Being a Christian means that I am called upon to do battle against lies, injustice, cruelty, hypocrisy."
3. "I have never liked France or the French, and I have never stopped saying so."
4. "We must attack France. What are they going to do?"
5. "Don't pray. Learn to use guns."
6. "There's nothing like horrendous physical pain to quell angry fanatics."
7. "There is not a worse prostitute in politics. . . . He's an utterly amoral repulsive creature."
8. "Let's just call it for what it is. They're whores."

Answer Key: 1. Hitler 2. Coulter 3. Hitler 4. Coulter 5. Coulter 6. Coulter 7. Hitler 8. Coulter

For discussion: What is the sound of no Anns yapping?

BATHHOUSE ANNIE

ANN SAYS: "Bill Clinton has latent homosexual tendencies."

WE SAY: Then you might have a chance with him after all.

• • • • • • • • • • • • •

ANN SAYS: Clinton's behavior "is reminiscent of a bathhouse."

WE SAY: Coulter's behavior is reminiscent of a haunted house.

• • • • • • • • • • • • •

ANN SAYS: "[Clinton] may not be gay, but Al Gore, total fag."

WE SAY: Did you bump into him at The Manhole?

• • • • • • • • • • • • •

ANN SAYS: "You know, when I tour college campuses, I always find the prettiest girls in the room are the ones in the College Republicans."

WE SAY: Why is Ann checking out the prettiest girls?

"I always find the prettiest girls. . . ."

Confessions of an al-Pieda Terrorist

After more than two years of public silence, Phillip Edgar Smith decided to speak. Along with William Zachary Wolff, Smith gained instant notoriety in 2004 for throwing pies at Ann during a speech at the University of Arizona. The two were immediately identified as members of al-Pieda—a previously unknown terrorist organization that upon exhaustive investigation was revealed to be a two-member group whose operatives, Phil and Zach, concealed themselves in student housing and apartments near the college.

Ann wrote about her terrifying brush with whipped cream in an April 15, 2005, column. She was outraged that the terrorists, though apprehended by authorities, went unpunished by the courts. Since then al-Pieda has vanished from the landscape and out of the public's consciousness. I concluded that the operatives were either (a) hiding from the U.S. Department of Homeland Security while plotting another strike against Ann[6]; (b) rotting behind barbed wire in Guantánamo; or (c) at home, watching *Gilmore Girls*.

With visions of traveling to caves in mountainous

[6.] The experts on Fox News have said that some terrorist groups may go years between attacks.

regions of Afghanistan, I sought the whereabouts of al-Pieda's members. After a couple of minutes of intense Internet searching, I learned that Zach was teaching English to children in a remote South American village, and I found Phil at his home in the desert in the western United States. He picked up his phone on the second ring. Until then Phil had not spoken publicly about the incident.

Phillip Edgar Smith of al-Pieda

William Zachary Wolff of al-Pieda

Hey, are you the guy who threw a pie at Ann Coulter a few years ago?

[Laughs] Yeah.

Are you in hiding?

No, I just got home from work.

I'm from the Homeland Security Agency, and I'd like to talk to you about al-Pieda.

Funny. Who are you? Really?

I'm writing a book called I Hate Ann Coulter. *I want to hear about the origins of your terrorist organization, al-Pieda—*

There's no organization. It was just me and Zach.

Well, you're heroes to a lot of people.

Really?

A lot of people want to mess her up.

We didn't want to hurt her. We just wanted to get some whipped cream in her face.

Let's go back to the beginning. How did al-Pieda come together, and how did you hatch this plan?

Zach and I were really good friends at U of A. We lived across the street from each other. He'd already graduated, and I was a senior majoring in political science. One night we were at this girl's house, sitting on the porch, and Zach said, "Hey, Ann Coulter is giving a talk at the school. Do you think it would be funny if we made a pie and threw it at her?" I said, "Sounds like a good idea. We should do it."

And that was it?

A lot of people thought we hatched the plan in retaliation for what the Young Republicans had done when Michael Moore had spoken at the school earlier in the year. The Young Republicans had brought in a big drum, and they beat it every time Moore tried to make a point. But our action had nothing to do with Moore. I didn't even belong to the college's Democrats club. We simply considered Ann to be more comedian than political commentator. She was cheerleading the war in Iraq, which we were against. We thought a lot of what she said was despicable. We thought she deserved a pie in the face.

What kind of pie was it?

Tofu cream. Zach is a great vegetarian chef. He said, "I'm going to make tofu cream pies," and I said, "Cool."

How did you infiltrate the auditorium?

About a week before she came on campus, Zach and another girl got tickets. One of the girls was involved in drama, and she gave us pointers on the layout of the stage and the best way we might want to make it up on the stage.

Take me through the day of the attack.

Ann's speech was at Centennial Hall, the theater on campus. We got there early. One of the guys working there showed us where the guests arrived. We waited for Ann, but she was about an hour late, and when her car finally showed up, she got out and ran inside too fast for us to catch her. We each had a pie. As we waited, they melted and ran over our fingers. We licked our fingers, and we agreed that the pies, which we'd made a few hours earlier, were pretty tasty.

Then what?

We went inside and sat down. We listened to Ann's speech, and it was the same old Ann Coulter. Her biggest policy is the policy of hating people who disagree with her. As she took questions after the speech, Zach and I turned to each other and said, "All right, let's do it." We walked down the aisle on the far end of the theater. We passed an usher guarding the stage. We walked right by him, in fact. As we went up the stairs, we pulled out the pies, and then we started to run. Zach threw his pie, and it sailed over Ann. Then I threw mine and exited stage left. I didn't even find out if it hit her. Later I heard there was some cream on her dress.

In her column Ann wrote, "Fortunately, liberals not only argue like liberals, they throw like girls." Ouch.

You try throwing a melting pie while on the dead run. We were nervous. It's not like we practiced.

Then what happened?

Zach ran back into the audience. I ran to the left, backstage, and as I was running, a guy tackled me. Within seconds, the police were on me. They had Zach, too. They cuffed both of us. One of the officers got on his walkie-talkie and said he was calling the biohazard unit. I told him that the pies were tofu cream. He said with all the terrorism shit going on, they couldn't take chances.

Like salmonella in the meringue?

I suppose. But they didn't get the joke. We were arrested, taken to the station, and put in a holding tank. It was like a big living room. Then we got out. The blogs were full of misinformation. They had us getting beat up and sent to prison. They said Ann had a bodyguard who tried to kill anyone who got near her. Her supporters said they hoped we got a taste of homosexuality in prison.

Did you?

Not even a hug good-bye.

TOFU TERROR PIE

INGREDIENTS

Filling:
16 oz. tofu (silken)

2 c. sugar

Salt, to taste

¾ c. water (room temperature)

1 tsp. vanilla extract

¼ tsp. lemon juice

1 c. rice flour

Crust:
6 tbsp. melted butter

1¼ c. graham cracker crumbs

¼ c. sugar

DIRECTIONS

Crust:
Combine butter, graham cracker crumbs, and sugar. Press into a 9-inch pie pan, then refrigerate for 1 hour.

Filling:
Blend tofu in a food processor for 3 minutes. In a saucepan whisk rice flour into 3/4 cup water. Turn heat to medium and whisk until the slurry thickens to a paste. Add the paste to the tofu, as well as the sugar, vanilla, lemon juice, and salt, and blend to combine. Transfer the filling into the piecrust and refrigerate for 2 hours.

Throw at Ann Coulter.

Black Tuesday

It was Tuesday, June 6, 2006, and it was a big day for Harry Walther. Walther is a Philadelphia-based Internet radio host better known as Pastor Harry. For months he'd promised devotees of his DoomsDay Talk radio show and Web site that he was, on this day, finally going to reveal the identity of the Antichrist, aka "the Beast."

Pastor Harry had spent thousands of hours using Bible code to decipher the name and identity of the Antichrist, and he believed it would cause a stir.

It was 6/6/6, after all.

But then She-Devil Ann snatched the spotlight from him by choosing that once-in-a-millennium day to promote the release of her latest book, *Godless,* by going on the highest-rated morning show on TV and throwing poisoned darts at women whose husbands had been killed in the World Trade Center on 9/11.

It was a totally selfish move. Indeed, Walther was majorly pissed.

Only Ann seemed to consider the day a success.

Her appearance was a watershed moment for her and the *Today* show. Many media wags thought she'd never self-promote from inside Studio 1A ever again after calling Katie Couric "the affable Eva Braun of morning television" and comparing her to Nazi propagandist Joseph Goebbels. They were wrong. If the show's producers were truly on point, they would've booked Pastor Harry that morning and had him reveal the Antichrist live in the first half hour—now, that's great television!

Early that Tuesday morning, Ann sauntered into the *Today* show studio dressed in her teasingly small black cocktail dress as if it were 6:00 p.m. rather than 6:00 a.m. She went into makeup and then waited to be interviewed by Matt Lauer. The first guest of the day, Ann looked impatient as Matt opened the segment by asking about President Bush's declining approval rating among voters. Ann quickly rerouted that to her favorite catchall for nearly every issue: a ban on gay marriage. *Yes, Matt, voters may not be happy with the war in Iraq, but they're behind the president and Congress as far as preventing homosexuals from marrying.* One day she's just going to serve up the master plan: *We should invade their bars, kill their libidos, and convert them to celibacy[7].*

[7.] If conservatives were serious about ridding the world of gay sex, they would permit gay marriage. What ends a sex life like marriage?

She perked up when Matt segued into her book. "Now we're on a subject I want!" said Ann. Like a porn star, she knew her fans demanded new, different, and ever-more-outrageous variations on the same old theme, and like the pro that she is, she didn't disappoint them when Matt angled in for the money shot.

LAUER: Do you—do you believe everything in this book, do you believe everything in the book, or do you put some things in there just that cater to your base?

COULTER: No, of course I believe everything.

LAUER: All right, on the 9/11 widows and, in particular, a group that had been outspoken and critical of the administration: "These self-obsessed women seemed genuinely unaware that 9/11 was an attack on our nation and acted as if the terrorist attacks happened only to them. . . . They believed the entire country was required to marinate in their exquisite personal agony. Apparently, denouncing Bush was an important part of their closure process." And this part is—is the part I really need to talk to you about. "These broads are millionaires, lionized on TV and in articles about them, reveling in their status as celebrities and stalked by grief-arazzis. I've never seen people enjoying their husbands' death so much."

COULTER: Yes.

A few days later *Los Angeles Times* media critic Tim Ruttan, one of many writing about this jarring display of bad taste disguised as punditry aimed at selling books, compared Ann's appearance to pornography: "[Pornography] is hard to define but you know it when you see it." She was vulgar. The whole thing was ugly. If you didn't already hate her, she gave you reason.

"I'm a Republican. Ann Coulter does not speak for me," wrote B. Jay Cooper, former deputy press secretary to Presidents Ronald Reagan and George H. W. Bush and communications director of the Republican National Committee under four chairmen. "To me, Ann Coulter's exercise of her right to free speech is the political equivalent of yelling fire in a crowded theater. She crosses the line of decency."

"Perhaps her book should have been called 'Heartless,'" Senator Hillary Clinton said the next day. "I know a lot of the widows and family members who lost loved ones on 9/11. They never wanted to be a member of a group that is defined by the tragedy of what happened."

Hillary added that she found it "unimaginable that

anyone in the public eye could launch a vicious, mean-spirited attack" on these women who'd already suffered such enormous loss and pain.

Another prominent Republican registered disgust: "I was really stunned and I don't think it's at all fair or accurate," Governor George Pataki of New York said. "I have spoken with many, many grieving family members and the hurt is real, the pain is real, the suffering four and a half years later has not lessened to any appreciable degree."

Even Bill O'Reilly called her words "mean and counterproductive."

NOT SUCH A *GODLESS* WORLD AFTER ALL

When Ann skulked out of her Upper East Side apartment three days after slandering the 9/11 widows on the *Today* show, she found proof that there is karma. Take the following June 9, 2006, post on Gawker.com:

I stole a cab from Ann Coulter after seeing her come out of an apartment building on the Upper East Side. She didn't look happy, dressed in a yellow raincoat and hailing a cab and it was her dejected face that first caught my attention. . . . [W]hen I realized who it was, I decided I had to steal the cab even though I had nowhere to go.

When Annimals Attack

Hate is a crowded field. Unfortunately for Ann, a lot of the good targets have already been taken. Pat Robertson and Jerry Falwell have already gone after gays for "causing" AIDS. The Westboro Baptist Church, headed by Pastor Fred Phelps, in Topeka, Kansas, runs its God Hates Fags Web site and pickets funerals of gay and lesbian soldiers. Mel Gibson and his father, Hutton Gibson, have staked out the Jewish conspiracy theory and Holocaust denial turf. Here are some targets that are still open:

- Three-legged puppies
- Orphans
- Burn victims
- Organ transplant survivors
- The Dalai Lama
- Grandma
- ~~Widows~~
- ~~9/11 victims~~

For discussion: I heard that Ann Coulter is such a dick that Viagra makes her taller.

The Anntichrist

A few days after her *Today* show appearance Ann whooped it up with talk radio host Sean Hannity in Huntington, Long Island, the home of thirty-four people killed in the September 11 attacks. With her book atop the bestseller list, she reveled in the applause of a few hundred devotees. At one point a protestor handed her a letter that said her comments about the 9/11 widows "were a disgrace to the thousands who perished on that day." It also said that her depiction of those four women was a "nauseating misrepresentation of their struggle to keep the memory of what happened that day alive."

How did Ann respond? She ripped up the letter. Her fans cheered.

I hate her.

Part 2:

How to Get Rid of a
Political Bunny Boiler

Dumping Ann

Admittedly, Ann initially looked good on paper. Lawyer. Author. She's also, in the words of Al Franken, "a nutcase." And nutcases are usually fun in bed. We thought she was cute, even sexy. We were turned on when she mewed, "Clinton is in love with the erect penis." Yes, it was disrespectful, but that mouth of hers was sassy and always ready for action.

Unfortunately, she became America's fatal attraction, a political "bunny boiler." But by the time she insulted the widows on the *Today* show, the Cult of Coulter felt icky. She talked about murder more than Charles Manson did: Murder Clinton. Murder journalists. Murder Arabs. Blow up the *Times* building. She made us feel like Squeaky Fromme.

We felt bad, lost, used, and abused. We had an epiphany: We wanted out.

The problem was, she wasn't done with us. She wouldn't let us go.

It officially became a problem relationship.

Our international friends and family of allied

nations tried to talk to us about our obsession with Ann. They attempted numerous interventions and "carefrontations," but we couldn't seem to let her go. To be fair, neither would she leave us alone. Every time we turned on the television, she was there. She was at the bookstore, in the newspaper, and on the Internet (nice going, Gore). She was always in our faces, promoting the glory days of McCarthyism and dishing out slander like a crazy cafeteria lady.

Back when the world was a simpler place, the only issue in America seemed to be chastising Clinton for receiving the world's most unpopular blow job. Ann had a role to play: add gasoline to the fire while looking very nearly attractive. Except for the man-hands and the Adam's apple, she was very acceptable. Nothing a scarf and two puppets couldn't hide. There's a reason politics is called "show business for ugly people," and Ann was not only a comparative looker, but fresh meat on the national stage.

But then Clinton left the White House, and she kept at it. Unrelentingly. Like a soldier in a time of peace, she had outlived her mission and become a danger, a trained killer with no enemy. So she had to create enemies; she spewed insanity on MSNBC, *Rivera Live, The O'Reilly Factor, Hannity & Colmes, Politically Incorrect,* and in her daily syndicated column. She torched the ground in the *New York Times,* on the cover of *Time* magazine, on Salon.com, and in the *Washington Post.* No subject was off-limits, no individual too sacred to berate, no race or ethnicity on a par with her WASP coven. She wooed America to the right—the irrational Far Right. She told us what to think, whom to like, whom to hate. She had America consigned to the idea that George W. Bush was brilliant and that terrorism, global warming, and soaring gasoline prices could be solved with a ban on gay marriage.

However, despite the current state of the world—daily death tallies of American soldiers, a steady parade of flag-waving corporate executives and Republican congress-people going to prison—America can recover from its bad choices if we choose to break it off with Ann. Once we dump her, we won't watch Fox News unless we feel like it. We'll begin to ask ourselves, *What liberal media bias?* We'll laugh at Ann's argument that Darwin's theory of evolution is a liberal creation myth. We'll buy pita bread again.

It'll be a brand-new life.

I Hate Ann Coulter, and So Do You

I hate Ann Coulter.

There. I said it.

Now I want you to try it. First silently, so no one else can hear. Once you get used to hearing those words coming out of your mouth, say them out loud. *I hate Ann Coulter.* Then say them to a friend or family member. Watch his face, note his reaction. Finally, summon your courage and open a window or walk out onto the street and say them to a stranger. *I hate Ann Coulter.*

With conviction.

If you happen by homeless people on the street holding up signs asking for money, ask them if they'd like some change. If they say yes, change their signs to read I HATE ANN COULTER!

MELANNOMA

Ann Coulter is like a painful lump that you discover in the shower. If you felt that under your arm or in your breast, you'd race to the doctor. He'd deliver the news gloomily:

The good news is that it's not cancer, he'd say. *The bad news is that it is Ann Coulter.*

Will she kill me?

Only if you're a liberal. But if you're a right-leaning moderate, she can make you very, very sick over time.

A Thousand Points of Light

By announcing that we hate Ann Coulter, we are actually engaging in a patriotic act as vital and significant as picking up a musket in 1776, getting shot at Kent State, or not flushing a number one during a drought.

All great movements start with simple acts by individuals. Consider:

- Patrick Henry vowing, "Give me liberty or give me death!"
- Rosa Parks refusing to change seats
- Jenny Craig telling you to start your diet today—what have you got to lose?
- You declaring, *I hate Ann Coulter!*

The only difference between Ann and the psycho on the sidewalk muttering obscenities and yelling at passersby is that Ann gets booked on the *Today* show. She is 120 unwanted pounds dragging America down. As individuals and as a nation, we know certain things are bad for us: cigarettes, fatty foods, hydrogenated oils, asbestos, unprotected anal sex, and Ann Coulter. Let's fulfill our national obligation to hate her as much as we hate anything destructive to this great country, and as vocally as possible.

Even Ann's paying customers are reaching the end of their tolerance, as seen in this review on amazon.com by "Book Lover" from Norman, Oklahoma:

> I agreed with several things discussed in the book and it was worth reading. However, there were times she seemed extremely petty and there were too many personal attacks for example "rabid widows" concerning 9/11. That was unnecessary. That is why I only gave it three stars.

Book Lover may not be where we are now, openly declaring that she hates Ann Coulter. But her review reveals dissent in the ranks of Ann loyalists. They, too, will join us in time.

Jimmy Carter Will Beat Your Ass

Ann makes the wonderfully deranged contention in *Godless* that a liberal, when questioned, "might turn violent—much like the practitioners of Islam, the Religion of Peace, who ransacked Danish embassies worldwide because a Danish newspaper published cartoons of Mohammed."

With her line of reasoning, one may conclude that former president Jimmy Carter, a Noble Prize–winning liberal, might be out to get R. W. Haferl Jr. of Fenwick Island, Delaware. Mr. Haferl Jr., an ordinary citizen, reviewed the gentle-spoken Georgian's most recent book, *Our Endangered Values,* on amazon.com, posting his thoughts on June 13, 2006. He gave the book only one out of five stars: "If you were trapped in a cave and need[ed] some paper to start a fire then buy this book," he wrote none too favorably. "Save your money."

Ouch.

I looked up Mr. Haferl and found him on the beach with his family on the Fourth of July.

"It wasn't much of a review," Mr. Haferl said.

"It was a dis nonetheless," I replied.

"A friend gave me the book. I didn't buy it," he said. "But I thought I'd give it a try. It was the same old, same old. I didn't like it."

"Are you at all concerned about Jimmy Carter showing up outside your house to deliver a major ass-whoopin'?" I asked.

"Nope," he said.

"But according to Ann Coulter, if you criticize or question a liberal, he may come after you. Violently."

"Jimmy Carter is incapable of violence," Mr. Haferl said. "He proved that when he was president. He's a lot older now."

"So you aren't on red alert for a peanut farmer with jihad in his eyes?"

"Nope. The kids are safe."

Let My People Go

If you recall the biblical Moses, he stood on the banks of the Nile and explained to the Pharaoh of Egypt that horrendous plagues would smite down his people because he would not let the Israelites go[8]. It took a miraculous warning and ten plagues before Pharaoh would accept that the Jews were getting out of Dodge. In the case of Ann the Unfairoh, we've got to remove eleven plagues before she will "let our people go":

1. *Serpents:* In the Bible, as a "miraculous sign of warning" to Pharaoh, Aaron's staff turned into a serpent. The opposite miracle will have to happen in the struggle against Ann: Media serpents must turn into competent and ethical newsroom staffs.

2. *Blood:* Once blood stops routinely turning to oil, Ann will be terrified that America is abandoning her doctrine that "conservation is the explicit abnegation of man's dominion over the Earth."

3. *Frogs:* America will stop hating the French and embrace them for what they are: our cheese-eating,

---

[8.] Check it out in *The Ten Commandments* starring Charlton Heston, actor and former NRA president; other credits include *Planet of the Apes* and *Soylent Green*.

surrender monkey allies, not the enemies that Ann suggested "we've got to attack" in her December 2001 column.

4. *Bugs:* America will quell the bugs used for warrantless eavesdropping authorized by President Bush—an action Ann defended.

5. *Wild Animals:* On the June 20, 2001, *Hannity & Colmes* episode that aired on Fox News, Ann famously said, "I take the biblical idea. We have dominion over the plants, the animals, the trees. God said, 'Earth is yours. Take it. Rape it. It's yours.'" If America would be willing to take a short break from sexually assaulting animals and trees, Ann might acknowledge her waning influence.

6. *Pestilence:* Purge the parasites by deleting Ann's column from your computer, removing bookmarks to NewsMax.com, the Drudge Report, the *Washington Times,* and FOXNews.com, including your RSS feeds[6]. Also, replace your Ann Coulter screen saver with a photo of your family or a puppy.

7. *Boils:* Write a letter to the makers of Abreva, asking them to research a pill that will shorten the healing time for "Ann Cold Sore."

8. *Hail of Fire:* Desert Storms may be "shock and awesome," but like *The Godfather* trilogy, only the first two were any good—let's stop while we're ahead.

---

[9] Keep your Shep Smith doll; your Anderson Cooper doll needs company.

9. *Grasshoppers:* Ignore the temptation to listen when Ann says, "Why not come and sing with me instead of conserving so hard?"

10. *Darkness:* End the darkness by donating your black cocktail dress to Goodwill. Keep the receipt for your taxes.

11. *Death:* Put a copy of *I Hate Ann Coulter* in your window so that harmful forces will "pass over" your home, leaving you and your family alone.

What's So Funny About War, Hate, and Condescension?

SHE SAYS: "Liberals refuse to condemn what societies have condemned for thousands of years—e.g., promiscuity, divorce, illegitimacy, homosexuality."

WE SAY: This is why liberals are invited to more parties.

SHE SAYS: "In the history of the nation, there has never been a political party so ridiculous as today's Democrats. It's as if all the brain-damaged people in America got together and formed a voting bloc."

WE SAY: Not all Democrats, just the ones who voted for Ralph Nader.

SHE SAYS: "I think we ought to nuke North Korea right now just to give the rest of the world a warning. . . . I just think it would be fun to nuke them and have it be a warning to the rest of the world."

WE SAY: Or we could just drop Ann into North Korea and let that be the lesson to the rest of the world.

SHE SAYS: "I have to say I'm all for public flogging."

WE SAY: Fox television already has this in development; it's called *So You Think You Can Flog?*

Photo copyright © 2006 Photodisc Green/Getty. Image of Ann copyright © 2006 Mike Stark, www.callingallwingnuts.com.

Teaching the world a lesson

SHE SAYS: "Then there are the 22 million Americans on food stamps. And of course there are the 39 million greedy geezers collecting Social Security."

WE SAY: Without those 61 million people, we wouldn't have daytime television!

SHE SAYS: "If the Democrats want to stay in the middle of the road, why do they keep sticking with Teddy Kennedy? Didn't he have some trouble staying in the middle of the road?"

WE SAY: Did Leno turn down this joke before you took it?

SHE SAYS: "I think our motto should be, post-9/11: Raghead talks tough, raghead faces consequences."

WE SAY: Our motto should be, post–*Nanny 911*: Ann says "raghead," Ann gets ragged on.

SHE SAYS: "There is no surer proof of Christ's divinity than that he is still so hated two thousand years after his death."

WE SAY: Ann will be hated in two thousand years, but she'll still just be a second-rate transvestite, not Divine.

SHE SAYS: The book *Anna Karenina* "really is just a brilliant take on human nature, being able to get into different people's perspectives."

WE SAY: What would Ann know about different people's perspectives?

SHE SAYS: "It's no fun riding around in those dinky little hybrid cars."

WE SAY: Ann, think of it as a mode of transportation, not as an extension of your penis.

SHE SAYS: "I get up at noon and work in my underwear."

WE SAY: Don't sit on her furniture until it's checked out with a black light.

SHE SAYS: "You could listen to the same songs at a hundred different Dead shows and it would sound different."

WE SAY: If only she'd sound different just *once*.

Canada to Ann: *Je vous deteste!*

Why should 32.5 million Canadians hate Ann? Because she hates them. Forget for a moment that we got Neil Young and Pamela Anderson from them. In late 2004, she began trashing our country's largest trade partner. "Canada has become trouble recently," she said on CNN. Did they want Tom Green back? Were they blasting Gordon Lightfoot's "The Wreck of the Edmund Fitzgerald" at us? Despite the mysterious root of her anger, Ann kept at it:

- "[Canadians] better hope the United States does not roll over one night and crush them. They are lucky we allow them to exist on the same continent."
- "We could have taken them over so easy. But I only want the western part, with the ski areas, the cowboys, and the right wingers. They're the only good parts of Canada."
- "It's always the worst Americans who go there."

Asked why she's so pissed at Canada, Ann said, "Because they speak French." She wants the Canadians to make English their official language, switch their flag insignia to a fig leaf, make the Grateful Dead's "Casey Jones" the national anthem, and change the spelling of their country's name to Cannada. Word of advice for Canada: Ignore her. As with terrorists and maniacs, you cannot negotiate with morons.

Do Ann's Books Cause Global Warming?

Every year that she publishes a book, the earth's temperatures hit record levels with detrimental effects. Look at the facts, draw your own conclusions. . . .

- **1998** *High Crimes:* The hottest year on record.
- **2002** *Slander:* The second-hottest year on record; wildfires scorched the West.
- **2003** *Treason:* The third-hottest year on record; extreme heat waves caused more than twenty thousand deaths in Europe.
- **2004** *How to Talk to a Liberal:* Among the hottest years on record; glaciers melted at alarming rates.
- **2006** *Godless:* The warmest first half of any year since records began in 1895.

Scientific reports show the United States with higher emissions than China, India, and Japan combined—most of them coming from Ann Coulter.

VARIATIONS ON "I HATE ANN COULTER"

"In soccer they score about as often as Ann Coulter makes sense."

>—BRYANT GUMBEL,
>*Real Sports with Bryant Gumbel*

". . . like with a Fellini movie, the deeper you get, the less sense Ann makes."

>—JONAH GOLDBERG, *National Review*

"Bill Clinton told Ann Coulter he was gay only to explain why he wasn't hitting on her bony ass."

>—*Late Night with David Letterman*

"Coulter's accusations have been as effectively discredited as Hitler's diaries."

>—ERIC ALTERMAN, *The Nation*

"In Coulter's beloved country there is no place for debate, only conformity."

>—JOE CONASON, *Salon.com*

"Without the total package, Ms. Coulter would be just one more nut living in Mom's basement."

>—DAVID CARR, *New York Times*

Students Risk Being Called "Ugly Gay Fetus Killers"

🖊 In December 2005, Ann got only fifteen minutes into a speech at the University of Connecticut before students interrupted with chants of "You suck!" Ann responded by saying, "I love to engage in repartee with people who are stupider than I am." So that's why she's always a guest of Sean Hannity!

🖊 Within two minutes of her February 23, 2006, "Liberals Are Wrong About Everything" speech at Indiana University, a student yelled, "Go back to Germany."

Note to friends and family of the student Republicans who supported Ann at these events: Wise up! While well-adjusted students have been doing bong hits and keg stands, your spawn in higher education have been greedily reading Ann's books, compulsively looking up her columns, and squandering all their money to hear her speak. They are addicts! They need your help!

Dame Coulter?

Have you ever seen Ann Coulter and Ted Nugent together? Go ahead, search Google images—nada. Both are right-wing media commentators, yet they have never been seen together. What are the chances of that? Both are thin and blond, their rhetoric is indistinguishable. Ted Nugent is a confessed sex addict, and you know how an addiction can escalate into more and more extreme behaviors. Is it so unlikely that he would try cross-dressing, just for a new kick? And from there, is it such a stretch to posit that Ann Coulter is really just Ted Nugent in a dress?

POP QUIZ: ANN COULTER OR TED NUGENT?

Identify the source of the following statements: Ann Coulter or Ted Nugent.

1. "It all gets down to the fact that all those who criticize me are a bunch of hippies and hypocrites. . . . Mostly, my critics are just idiots."

---

2. "I think the government should be spying on all Arabs, engaging in torture as a televised spectator sport, dropping daisy cutters wantonly throughout the Middle East, and sending liberals to Guantánamo."

3. "We should put razor wire around our borders."

4. "About national health care: The government must stay out of my life."

5. "If they have the one innocent person who has ever to be put to death this century out of over 7,000, you probably will get a good movie deal out of it."

6. "[Hillary Clinton's] very existence insults the spirit of individualism in this country."

Answer Key: 1. Nugent **2.** Coulter **3.** Nugent **4.** Nugent **5.** Coulter **6.** Nugent

---

THE ANN COULTER MOVIE GUIDE

Desperately Seeking Attention

Starr Whores

Get Frank Rich or Lie Tryin'

Do the Ultra-Right Thing

Jerks 2

Good Bill Hunting

The Blair Bitch Project

Bill and Ted's Sexual Adventures

Snakes on a Panel

She's the Man

How to Talk to Ann (If You Must)

If Ann senses the potential to sell books, she will give you an interview. The only outlet she hasn't yet spoken to is Al Jazeera[10]. On her Web site she has the temerity to list writers to whom she will speak again, including John Cloud from *Time* magazine and Taylor Hill of jam-bands.com. Those not invited back comprise a much longer and more prestigious list. On the condition of anonymity, one of those journalists spoke about the experience of talking to Ann.

What was it like talking to Ann?

I'm still recovering, and it's been a year. No, seriously, I washed my hands thoroughly and felt like I got rid of the grime. I liked the description in the *L.A. Times*: that she's the adopted love child of Oscar Wilde and Gore Vidal, but only the idea she was raised by gays, which would offer some insight. But I think of her as the spawn of Joan Rivers and Scott Peterson. She is quick, clever, and pathological.

Does she really believe everything she says?

She loves hearing herself talk. She's enamored by her own cleverness. If it works for her, meaning if it sells books or gets her more attention that sells more books, she believes it. Otherwise, she's Cheney in a dress—the straight daughter he never had.

---

[10] A search for Ann Coulter on aljazeera.net produces 0 results.

What motivates her?

Ann is in this business to make money. If she found out tomorrow that liberals sell more books, she'd be on Air America faster than you can say "Sean Hannity." She's like every other Republican—she wants to make money. That's where the liberals messed up. They have causes they believe in.

Does she say some things just to shock people and get quoted?

Does Pamela Anderson wear bikinis? Getting quoted is her business—the more the better. She knows the value of blood and guts.

Having spent time with her, how would you describe her, politically speaking?

Your typical conservative: a narrow-minded, God-obsessed psychopathic killer. And, as she'd say, those are her good traits.

How can you generalize like that?

Maybe not all conservatives are narrow-minded, God-obsessed psychopathic killers. But all narrow-minded, God-obsessed psychopathic killers are conservatives.

What does Ann ultimately want?

More book sales, more attention, more money, and more fame.

What does she want for America?

To transform it into her hometown, New Canaan, Connecticut. It's 93 percent Caucasian, conservative, and Christian. She's hung up on C-words.

Speaking of C-words . . .

"Coulter" is a C-word too. Although given her master-race ideals, it may be better to spell that with a "K."

What will be her legacy?

While she sees herself as the successor to William F. Buckley and George Will, she's closer to a political Jenna Jameson. She's the porn star for conservatives. She'll leave a body of work, emphasis on "body."

What's her greatest accomplishment thus far?

She's kept her clothes on. Thank goodness.

Liberal Education

Dear Bill Clinton,

I am writing a book called *I Hate Ann Coulter*. Do you have anything to add?

Sincerely,

Unanimous

From the Desk of William J. Clinton

Dear Unanimous,

Please find out why she called me a "latent homosexual." How can she make comments like those when she hasn't sampled Bubba's barbecue?

Best of luck,

Bill

P.S. A CDC file labeled ANN COULTER: HERPES/CONFIDENTIAL will be on the front seat of your car tomorrow.

P.P.S. Do you have a phone number for that skinny little tramp?

Dear Al Gore,

I am writing a book called *I Hate Ann Coulter.* Do you have anything to add?

Sincerely,

Unanimous

From the Desk of Al Gore

Dear Unanimous,

Even if I weren't a "total fag," I wouldn't bang her with Bill's dick.

Very truly yours,

Al

Dear U.S. Senator Hillary Clinton,

I am writing a book called *I Hate Ann Coulter.* Do you have anything to add?

Sincerely,

Unanimous

From the Desk of Senator Hillary Rodham Clinton

Dear Unanimous,

You don't just play field hockey with someone and then never call again. She should call her next book *Heartless*!

Sincerely,

Hillary

New Canaan Syndrome

Poor Jonah Goldberg. Just look at how the editor-at-large of National Review Online struggles and wrestles and justifies his decision to drop Ann Coulter:

Goldberg says: "[She] wrote a long, rambling rant of a response to her critics that was barely coherent. Running this 'piece' would have been an embarrassment to Ann, and to NRO."

We say: Goldberg, running every "piece" by her was an embarrassment all along!

Goldberg says: "Ann didn't fail as a person—as all her critics on the Left say—she failed as a WRITER, which for us is almost as bad."

We say: Ann failed as a mammal, Goldberg. She failed as an organic life-form!

Goldberg: "What publication on earth would continue a relationship with a writer who would refuse to discuss her work with her editors?"

We say: *Der Stürmer?*

Goldberg: "We did not 'fire' Ann for what she wrote, even though it was poorly written and sloppy. We ended the relationship because she behaved with a total lack of professionalism, friendship, and loyalty."

We say: Jonah, get over it! When it comes to dumping Ann, NO JURY WOULD CONVICT YOU!

In and Out of Love

In her forties, Ann has been engaged at least three times. "Something like that," she said. Let's look at some of her past relationships:

DINESH D'SOUZA

Occupation:	Conservative writer
Attraction:	Ann was taller than him
Reason for split:	Too cheesy, fattening

BOB GUCCIONE JR.

Occupation:	Publisher
Attraction:	Ann was taller than him
Reason for split:	Various pet projects, pet issues, and pet peeves

BILL MAHER

Occupation:	Comedian
Attraction:	Ann was taller than him
Reason for split:	Neither would share the mirror

How to Talk Like a Porn Star

"Despite my claims to secrecy, the last three or four boyfriends I have had are people that I met because I bumped into them on the street."

"Let's say I go out every night, I meet a guy and have sex with him. Good for me. I'm not married."

"I date, but from there I will be as honest as Bill Clinton was under oath."

"You can look and look and look, but there is actually nothing in the Constitution about sodomy. It doesn't forbid sodomy."

"I am emboldened by my looks to say things Republican men wouldn't[11]."

Rev. Jerry Falwell: "I think Ann is a brilliant girl, and she's got the quickest mouth in the East."

---

[11] For example, "How do you like my Johnson administration?"

"[The Constitution] doesn't forbid sodomy."

On Being Ann Coulter

She's the most famous, but she's not the only Ann Coulter. There are dozens of Ann Coulters across the United States. "I'm a bleeding heart liberal biochemist, the polar opposite of her," says Ann Coulter of Baton Rouge, Louisiana. "It's not fun, and it's only gotten worse as she's gotten worse."

Ann Coulter of Avon, Ohio, isn't any happier about the situation. "A lot of people prank call me," she says.

Another Ann Coulter, from the Midwest, says she wishes she could buy a vowel. "Sometimes I'll lie in bed and wonder if my life would be any different if I had an 'e,' if I was A-n-n-e Coulter. I've thought about changing it legally. My husband thinks I'm nuts. He says it wouldn't make a difference because the 'e' is silent."

"I wasn't always Ann Coulter," says another. "It's my married name. It was fine for the first seventeen years of our marriage. But then this—I don't even know what to call her—came on the scene and ruined my name."

"Thank God for the 'a' at the end of my name," says Anna Coulter from her home on the West Coast. "I'd hate to be Ann Coulter. I'd change my name. The way it is now is too close already."

Femannism

She says: "Anorexics never have boyfriends. That's one way to know you don't have anorexia, if you have a boyfriend."

We say: Ann, *you* don't have a boyfriend! And even if you get one, you'll still be Ano.

She says: "My pretty-girl allies stick out like a sore thumb amongst the corn-fed, no makeup, natural fiber, no-bra needing, sandal-wearing, hirsute, somewhat fragrant hippie chick pie wagons they call 'women' at the Democratic National Convention."

We say: You can be our wingman anytime, Ann! No fat chicks! Wooooo!

She says: "I think [women] should be armed but should not vote. . . . [W]omen have no capacity to understand how money is earned. They have a lot of ideas on how to spend it . . . it's always more money on education, more money on child care, more money on day care."

We say: Aha! We knew you were a man!

Coultourettes

Bill Maher: "[Ann] absolutely never pulls a punch. Even when she's saying something that I think is outrageous. . . . And that is what I find so refreshing and, unfortunately, so unique. I can't name five other people who do that, who don't calculate before they speak."

Gee, Bill, you must not be trying very hard. Just off the tops of our heads, we came up with:

1. Mel Gibson
2. Terrell Owens
3. Janice Dickinson
4. John Rocker
5. Britney Spears
6. Courtney Love
7. Charles Barkley
8. Pat Robertson
9. Kim Jong Il
10. Ted Turner
11. Jerry Lewis
12. Bill Maher

Oops, that's twelve already, but who's counting?

Half Baked

Promoting *Godless* on the Christian Broadcasting Network's *The 700 Club,* Ann and host Gordon Robertson tore into Darwin's theory of evolution. Ann called it a "myth," a fabrication of the liberal religious code.

COULTER: They've never figured out how the eye could have evolved by natural mutation—random mutation and natural selection.

ROBERTSON: You're right. On a scientific basis, there's no fossil record of what transitional species or even transitional—you know, how did we get a bat wing?

COULTER: Right.

ROBERTSON: And we just seem to ignore that, conveniently.

COULTER: Well, they have little stories about how a bear fell into the ocean and became a whale. But we don't have the actual bear and the whale.

Whoa! We were blown away by what we heard on two counts.

1. Just how friggin' good is the weed in the CBN studio?
2. Forget how we got bat wings—how do we get some Buffalo wings up in this bitch?

COULTER: They have species that could, in theory, be a transition between one animal and another. But as I say in the book, this is like saying, you know, Elton John looks like Janet Reno. Therefore, Elton John gave birth to Janet Reno.

Ann, using this logic, you would actually deny that k.d. lang gave birth to Clay Aiken. Stop making a fool of yourself! And pass the dutchie!

Still not convinced that Ann is high? How about what she wrote in *Godless*: "Imagine a giant raccoon passed gas and perhaps the resulting gas might have created the vast variety of life we see on Earth."

Ann, there's a time and a place for everything, and it's called "college." Put down the pipe and get a real job.

WE D.A.R.E. YOU

Kids, drugs are bad, mmmmmmkay? Just ask Rush
Limbaugh about the dangers of OxyContin or Bob Dole
about Viagra abuse (on second thought, ask his wife). But
there is one drug that might be good for Ann: Sodium
Pentothal. For once, she would tell the truth! Or would she
just melt like the Wicked Witch of the West?

'Taint corn. It's dope!

Darwin/Win

She says: "No one disputes that a monkey looks like a human, especially in the case of Al Franken."
We say: Ann shows us where we got weasels.

She says: "Liberals' creation myth is Charles Darwin's theory of evolution, which is about one notch above Scientology in scientific rigor."
We say: That puts it two notches above Ann's books.

She says: Evolution is "the false science."
We say: Ann proves de-evolution is very real.

COULTERCARD	
Treason in hardcover	$26.95
Ann Coulter talking doll	$29.95
Booking Ann to speak	$25,000
A universe with Ann Coulter in it	*Godless*

Brassball

Here's an exchange between MSNBC *Hardball* host Chris Matthews and Ann while she was promoting *Godless* on his show on July 21, 2006.

Opening salvo:

MATTHEWS: The question I have is, **Do you have a soul?**

Later:

COULTER: Could we do something we haven't done on this book tour yet, and that's talk about the book rather than the words I use?

MATTHEWS: Well, the problem is, **the way I read is I go by the words.**

Ann Coulter-Robertson
Mrs. Ann Robertson-Coulter
Ann and Pat Robertson
The Robertsons

Do you believe in soul mates? The 1980 Kenny Rogers hit "Coward of the County" promises "There's someone for everyone," even you, Ann. As we all know, eHarmony's compatibility matching has produced many loving, lasting relationships. This is because eHarmony matches couples based on shared values. Let's see how Ann Coulter and Pat Robertson match up.

RELIGIOUS TOLERANCE

ROBERTSON: "You say you're supposed to be nice to the Episcopalians and the Presbyterians and the Methodists and this, that, and the other thing. Nonsense. I don't have to be nice to the spirit of the Antichrist."

COULTER: "The Episcopalians don't demand much in the way of actual religious belief. They have girl priests, gay priests, gay bishops, gay marriages—it's much like the *New York Times* editorial board."

VIOLENCE

ROBERTSON: "What we need is for somebody to place a small nuke at Foggy Bottom [headquarters of the State Department]."

COULTER: "My only regret was that Timothy McVeigh didn't hit the *New York Times* building."

MUSLIMS

ROBERTSON: "These people are crazed fanatics, and I want to say it now, I believe it's motivated by demonic power, it is satanic and it's time we recognize what we're dealing with. . . . And by the way, Islam is not a religion of peace."

COULTER: Said "not all Muslims are terrorists, but all terrorists are Muslims" and ". . . Muslims immediately engage in acts of mob violence when things don't go their way."

EDUCATION

ROBERTSON: Accused liberal professors of being "racists, murderers, sexual deviants and supporters of Al-Qaeda."

COULTER: Described public school teachers as "taxpayer-supported parasites."

Only one thing lasts longer than blood diamonds, Ann, and that's true love. It's bigger than the both of you.

YOU'RE TOO INTO ANN IF . . .

1. You quit your lucrative NASCAR driving career because you can't stand turning left.

2. You considered passing the dutchie on the right-hand side but then decided to just keep it for yourself.

3. You think Tim LaHaye's *Left Behind* must be liberal erotica.

4. You ask your wife or girlfriend to wear a short black dress and a blond wig.

5. You ask your husband or boyfriend to wear a short black dress and a blond wig.

6. You ask Ann if she'll donate her sperm to fertilize your eggs.

7. You still believe in the power of prayer—even though millions have been praying for Ann to shut up, to no avail.

INNER BEAUTY

Ann says: "So which women are constantly being called ugly? Is it Maxine Waters, Chelsea Clinton, Janet Reno, or Madeleine Albright? No, none of these. Only conservative women have their looks held up to ridicule because only liberals would be so malevolent."

Then Ann says: "The only sort of authority Cindy Sheehan has is the uncanny ability to demonstrate, by example, what body types should avoid wearing shorts in public."

The Baby Seal Book Club

Because you shouldn't waste your time or money on Ann's books, here are the essentials distilled from all five of her efforts.

High Crimes and Misdemeanors: The Case Against Bill Clinton (1998)

Ann's first book, which includes allegedly plagiarized material, it goes after Clinton for his dalliance with Monica Lewinsky. She claims, "If Clinton stayed, we may as well change our national motto from 'In God We Trust' to the old Nike slogan: 'Just Do It.'" Well, that's exactly what George W. and Rumsfeld did, and look at us in Iraq now.

The book she should have written: *Contact Highs and Grilled Cheese Vendors: Casey Jones Is Still Truckin'*

Slander: Liberal Lies About the American Right (2002)

In the second paragraph she writes, "It's all liberals' fault," and that sums up the entire book. Branded "notorious for its errors and distortions of facts" by

Brendan Nyhan of spinsanity.com, this book is allegedly all Ann's own work.

The book she should have written: *Pander: Conservatives Buy When the Skirt Is Tight*

Treason: Liberal Treachery from the Cold War to the War on Terrorism (2003)

More of the same, but this time Ann sets her story in the 1950s and selects Senator Joseph McCarthy as the misunderstood, much maligned defender of America. *Treason* impressed critic Joe Conason as filled "with falsehoods and distortions, as well as so much plain bullshit." Though otherwise well researched, as evidenced by pages of endnotes, she fails to mention that McCarthy once defended Nazi SS officers accused of murdering American POWs.

The book she should have written: *Reseasoned: Flavorful Chicanery for Last Week's Soup Warmed Over Again*

How to Talk to a Liberal (If You Must) (2004)

This collection of columns written by a lonely woman up at 3:00 a.m. and working in her underwear can be read for free online by fellow insomniacs in their undies.

The book she should have written: *How to Hawk to a Conservative (With Your Bust)*

Godless: The Church of Liberalism (2006)

All the same characters return—Bill and Hillary, Ted Kennedy, and so forth. Includes a lengthy ridicule of Darwin and evolutionary theory based on pseudo-science and discredited sources, as well as her famous attack on the 9/11 widows, which will forever mark the beginning of her end.

The book she should have written: *Guyless: The Crutch of Narcissism*

Point/Coulterpoint

We put some of Ann's claims about liberals to the test by phoning Jane Fleming, executive director of the Young Democrats of America, and asking her to respond to some of Ann's statements.

ANN SAYS: "Even Islamic terrorists don't hate America like liberals do."

FLEMING SAYS: "Come on, did she really say that?"

ANN SAYS: "Liberals are crazy."

FLEMING SAYS: "I think Ann Coulter is dying on the vine out there. Republicans have clearly cut and run from Ann. They've embraced Michelle Malkin. Maybe without the spotlight, Ann will start thinking straight."

Casting Ann Coulter

We called top Hollywood casting agents, said we were making a movie about Ann Coulter, and asked whom they'd cast as her. Here's what they said:

- Mary-Kate Olsen
- Kate Bosworth
- Keira Knightly
- Nicole Ritchie
- Mischa Barton
- Lindsay Lohan
- Kelly Ripa
- Karen Carpenter (exhumed)
- An upturned broom

> For discussion:
> Salon.com: Just to be mischievous—who is the most handsome conservative you can think of?
> Ann Coulter: Matt Drudge.

The Sound and the Furry

Mike Stark of callingallwingnuts.com and a pal pulled this picture from a video they took of Ann at a Freedom Alliance gathering hosted by Oliver North and Sean Hannity at New Jersey's Six Flags in July 2006. "When I got back home I looked at the video and was stunned to see how furry her face was," he says. "I immediately knew I had something special."

CAPTION THE PHOTO:

 $5 mustache rides

 Waxless

 Shave the date

 Matt Drudge, beard

Best. Interview. Ever.

Here's the transcript of Ann's July 7, 2006, appearance on Adam Carolla's syndicated radio show:

CAROLLA: Ann Coulter, who was supposed to be on the show about an hour and a half ago, is now on the phone as well. Ann?

COULTER: Hello.

CAROLLA: Hi, Ann. You're late, babydoll.

COULTER: Uh, somebody gave me the wrong number.

CAROLLA: Mmm . . . how did you get the right number? Just dialed randomly—eventually got to our show? [Laughter in background]

COULTER: Um, no. My publicist e-mailed it to me, I guess, after checking with you.

CAROLLA: Ahh, I see.

COULTER: But I am really tight on time right now because I already had a—

CAROLLA: All right, well, get lost. [Hangs up]

New Canaan High, Class of '80

JOHN: Ann was my first kiss. It was at a party. I said I combed my hair with a washcloth to look like Ronald Reagan, and she grabbed my head and kissed me. With tongue.

CARRIE: She suggested the prom theme should be "The Bitch Is Back." Instead, we went with "Forever Young."

HOLLY: We were on the fencing team together. She's very aggressive. She told me that she psyched herself up before matches by pretending the other team was Vietcong.

KELLY: We were both political. We started the Joshua Weintraub Is a Fag Club.

JILL: She was in my eleventh-grade American history class. One day I said that I supported Ronald Reagan's candidacy. Ann was my first kiss.

HASSAN: I was the only Middle Eastern kid at school. Ann came to our house one night and demanded my mother turn over all of our assets, including any Iranian caviar. Later I learned her parents were having a dinner party. When I got my driver's license, Ann told me it didn't apply to flying carpets. I hate her.

TEACHER: I had Ann in one of my classes, and I overheard her saying, "I love being taught by people stupider than I am."

CRAIG: I broke up with her after she said, "I love dating people who are uglier than I am."

TRACY: In all the years I went to school with her, she never blinked.

Male Bag

In July 2006, the *New York Times* received a letter containing a mysterious white powder. "Makes all of Ann Coulter's comments seem a little less funny," a *Times* source told *Women's Wear Daily* writer Jacob Bernstein, who then contacted Ann. Coulter's response? "So glad to hear that the *New York Times* got my letter." But she is not the only one who sends letters.

> Dear Ann,
>
> Luckily for you, Tony Soprano is a fictional character. However, he's based on some real people right here in Jersey. Take that for what you will.
>
> Best of luck,
>
> The Jersey Girls

> Dear Ann,
>
> Want to go for a ride sometime? I love late-night drives along the river.
>
> Let me know.
>
> Love,
>
> Teddy "Bear" Kennedy

Dear Ann,

How much do I owe you? I can't remember.

Tom DeLay

P.S. Please shred this note.

Babydoll,

I refilled my prescription.

What time? Where?

Rush

Hey Sugar Tits,

I'm on the lam from the Jews. Can I stay with you for a while?

Mel

Honey,

I saw you on TV the other day pushing your latest book, *Crotchless*, or whatever you called the damn thing. I didn't listen to a word you said, but I thought you looked phenomenal. I could hardly see your Adam's apple. I need to know who does your makeup. Please contact me.

Air kisses,

RuPaul

Can You Be Like Ann?

It takes more than an Ivy League education, a total lack of compunction, and the ability to plagiarize to be like Ann Coulter. You must also be a bitch. Can you cut it? Take the test.

1. Do you condemn everyone who disagrees with you, even though you contradict yourself often?
2. Do you have Nicorette in more than one orifice right now?
3. Do you find yourself holding court on ever-smaller cable channels and increasingly obscure Web sites?
4. Do you find yourself rejected by extremists for being "too extreme"?
5. Did you switch your favorite word from "betrayal" to "cruelty" because it has a nobler ring to it?
6. Does it bother you as a Christian that Jesus never kicked anyone's ass?

Results:

If you answered "yes" to all six questions, then you should be writing books and appearing on Fox News regularly. You probably already are.

THE BLAIR BITCH PROJECT

To make your own Ann Coulter voodoo doll[12], you'll need:

- A scallion
- A piece of black construction paper
- A potato

Step 1: Cut the construction paper into the shape of a minidress.

Step 2: Place it on top of the scallion.

Step 3: Make matchsticks from the potato for arms.

Step 4: Staple it all together.

Carry your voodoo doll around with you at all times. When people ask you what's that smell, show them your doll and say, "Ann Coulter stinks."

[12.] Sean Penn told the *New Yorker* that he has a plastic Ann Coulter doll that he likes to torture. "We violate her," Penn said. "There are cigarette burns in some funny places."

What Would Ann Do?

1. Your dog poops on your neighbor's lawn. What do you do?
   a. Publicly regret that he didn't do it inside the *New York Times* building
   b. Take the biblical idea: God gave us the earth. My dog can shit on it.
   c. Say that, frankly, you're not a big fan of the pooper-scooper laws
   d. All of the above

2. You are having a disagreement with a coworker. What do you do?
   a. Call him a terrorist
   b. Accuse him of masturbating in the sinks
   c. Spread rumors that he's a "total fag"
   d. All of the above

3. You're in the express line (ten or fewer items) at the grocery store and there's a Muslim ahead of you with eleven items. What do you do?
   a. Call the Department of Homeland Security on speed dial
   b. Invade his basket, spill his Cheetos, and convert him to Pirate's Booty
   c. Push ahead, shouting, "Raghead exceeds item limit, raghead suffers consequences!"
   d. All of the above

Answer Key: 1) d   2) d   3) d

Apocryphal Ann

Did you know that bashing Ann is nothing new? For nearly one hundred years our greatest literary lions have participated in this game of one-upmanship.

"The belief in a supernatural source of evil is not necessary; Ann Coulter alone is quite capable of every wickedness."

—JOSEPH CONRAD

"Ann is dangerous because she imagines herself pure in heart, for her purity, by definition, is unassailable."

—JAMES BALDWIN

"When good people in any country cease their vigilance and struggle, then Ann Coulter will prevail."

—PEARL S. BUCK

"At least two thirds of our miseries spring from Ann Coulter's stupidity, malice, and those great motivators and justifiers of malice and stupidity, idealism, dogmatism, and proselytizing zeal on behalf of religious or political idols."

—ALDOUS HUXLEY

Early Coulter Book Discovered

This rare manuscript was found in the Rye, New York, attic of a deceased literary agent.

By Dick Palmer

July 26, 2006

RYE, NY (AP)—What if Ann Coulter were more obsessed with her looks and finding Mr. Right than in serving as the air-raid siren for the right wing?

An unpublished book written by Ann Coulter gives a surprising impression of the pre-fame, pre-published, pre-Monicagate conservative pundit.

"Today it seems to me providential that Fate should have chosen blond as my hair color," she wrote in the book titled *Mein Coif* under the pseudonym Anndolf Coultler.

The manuscript was discovered in the Rye, NY, attic of a recently deceased literary agent who turned down Coulter's early effort.

"You write with force and passion," read a rejection letter from Mimi Lamb, the agent who turned down a young, ambitious Coulter. The agent offered to read a rewrite. In a postscript she also suggested that the young writer should wax her upper lip, but she warned that to do so would require a lifetime of maintenance.

"It'll grow back even thicker," she wrote.

Afterword: A Letter from Unanimous

Dear Readers,

I hope that you are enjoying the war in Iraq, global warming, and the cancellation of your pensions and 401(k)s. How I wish I could join you in the welfare lines, at the clinics while you wait for your abortions, or in the bars where you do body shots with the Kennedys. Alas, I have spent my summer vacation writing *I Hate Ann Coulter*.

If you have ever wondered what it's like to read all of Ann's books, columns, and commentary and even play with the Ann Coulter doll, I will tell you: It's like watching *Schindler's List*, but without the levity. I did it for us, America, so don't let me down. Give Ann the boot!

Sincerely,
Unanimous

Printed in the United States
By Bookmasters